HomeOwner's Guide

Information Everyone needs to know

A step-by-step guide to use before and after you take possession of your home!

David Erickson
Lori Gaston

Order this book online at www.trafford.com
or email orders@trafford.com

Most Trafford titles are also available at major online book retailers.

Print information available on the last page.

ISBN: 978-1-4251-1845-7 (sc)

Trafford rev. 05/19/2022

Trafford PUBLISHING® www.trafford.com

North America & international
toll-free: 844-688-6899 (USA & Canada)
fax: 812 355 4082

Dedication

The purchase of a house is typically the largest single financial transaction you will make. It is also a very emotional time. It's your dream. It's to be your "home".

This books seeks to find ways to save you time and provide convenience in addressing items within the home, prior to and after the purchase to avoid pitfalls, costly repairs, in essence to save you money. As you protect your home with the scheduled maintenance suggested, your home will make you money by building equity.

Don't be afraid to ask the questions. Knowledge of your home is a powerful tool and the equity you build secures your future.

A word from the Authors ...

With over 30 plus years combined experience in the construction industry and having owned/operated multiple businesses in the home building industry, we recognized the need for an informational tool to empower the homeowner/home buyer with the knowledge and the understanding to ask the right questions in an easy to use format.

Table of Contents

Congratulations on your decision to purchase this book! This book is intended for the new or resale homeowner and/or renter. It will give you valuable and concise information on how to assess the inner workings of your new residence, thereby providing you with the consumer awareness you need as you go through this exciting journey.

On the following pages, you will find a breakdown that takes you from room to room identifying items you should look for as you inspect your new or existing home. We have also provided examples and helpful hints in caring for your home as well as a section for notes in the back of this book. This book is a valuable tool for the ***Cosmetic Deficiency Warranty*** as outlined in the warranty section provided by your builder. It gives the resale homeowner and renter a way to assess their home. This book also assists you in properly maintaining your residence.

Typically, **for the new homeowner**, the builder's representative will meet you at the home for an orientation to explain the inner workings of your new home. The warranty will be explained as well as how to obtain warranty service from their company. Usually the builder has a set time limit per home when performing an orientation. By having a checklist and a set of preset questions for this day, your orientation will be smooth and free of distractions. You will find the questions you need to ask in this book as you go from room to room.

For the resale homeowner, you will be able to assess your new home like a pro. This book gives concise information which will enable you to check the inner workings of the home in an easy format.

For the renter, this book provides information to assist you in assessing the home for any minor deficiencies prior to moving in. This will help you secure your deposit when it is time to move to your next new home.

As you proceed through the book, you will notice that some of the words are **bold** and *italicized*. We have included definitions for these words in the back of this book, which will explain them in easy to understand layman terms.

Along with this book, bring the following items with you during your walk-through orientation as they will come in handy:

- **Pen:** You will want to use the checklists and note section for reference.

- **Small night light:** This will allow you to check the electrical outlets throughout the house.

- **Tape Measure:** In case you need to measure for window coverings, refrigerator or appliances, etc.

On the following pages you will find a chart for each specific **room** with the particular components for that room. We have also included pertinent questions for you to ask, which will provide you invaluable information about your home and help you determine whether or not corrective action is necessary on that particular item. If so, the item should be noted on your chart in that particular box (see sample chart below). All items noted require immediate correction prior to you taking possession or closing on your new home.

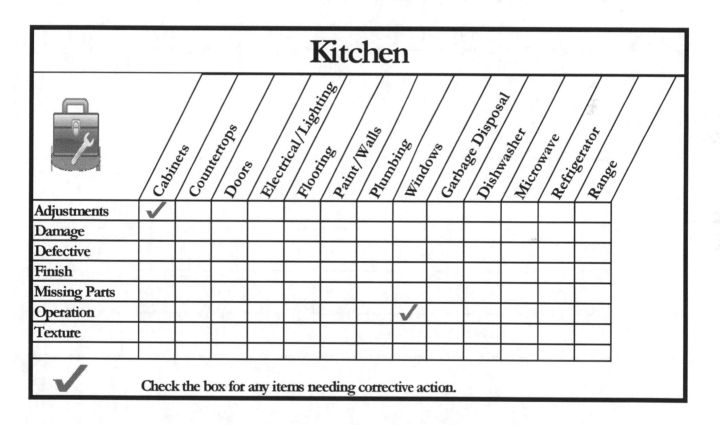

Kitchen

	Cabinets	Countertops	Doors	Electrical/Lighting	Flooring	Paint/Walls	Plumbing	Windows	Garbage Disposal	Dishwasher	Microwave	Refrigerator	Range
Adjustments	✓												
Damage													
Defective													
Finish													
Missing Parts													
Operation							✓						
Texture													

✓ Check the box for any items needing corrective action.

After the orientation or initial walk through of your home, review the list with the builder representative/seller so that he/she will be able to write down the items that need correction or replacement prior to taking ownership of the home. Always keep a copy of your findings on the house as well as a copy of the builders/seller corrections made and documented. This will ensure that there won't be any discrepancies upon the delivery of your home or the corrections that are needed.

Reminder: Bold and *italicized* words are defined in the back of this book.

4

Kitchen

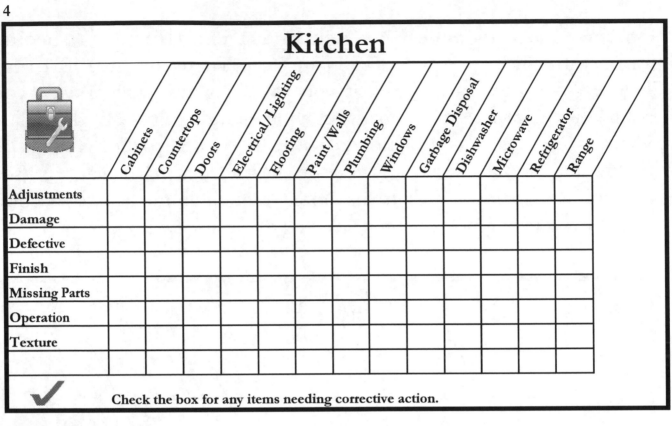

	Cabinets	Countertops	Doors	Electrical/Lighting	Flooring	Paint/Walls	Plumbing	Windows	Garbage Disposal	Dishwasher	Microwave	Refrigerator	Range	
Adjustments														
Damage														
Defective														
Finish														
Missing Parts														
Operation														
Texture														

Check the box for any items needing corrective action.

Notes:

_____

_____

_____

_____

_____

_____

_____

_____

_____

Kitchen:

- Is the texture on the walls and ceilings uniform in appearance? No noticeable repairs or *flashing of paint*?

- Do the doors open properly and close securely and lock? (You should not see any light coming from around the *exterior doors* when closed. Interior doors should open and close with ease and shut/lock securely.)

- Are there *GFCI's*?

- What is the *GFCI's* function?

- Use your nightlight to check each outlet to ensure it is working properly.

- Do all lights work (no burned out bulbs)?

- Do the *windows* slide open and close easily?

- Do the *windows* lock and unlock easily?

- Are window coverings installed and operating correctly?

- Are the *storm windows* and/or screens installed on the windows?

- Is the house *pre-wired for alarms* at exterior doors and windows? If so, do you see the *pre-wire alarm* button? If missing, have it noted on the chart as well as your builder/seller's paperwork for correction.

- Is the flooring free of any defects? (Refer to page 24—25 for more information)

- Are the countertops defect free?

- Are the warranty manuals and registration cards for the appliances supplied? What are the warranties on the appliances?

- Operate each appliance (i.e. refrigerator, icemaker, dishwasher, range, disposal, microwave.)

- If the microwave is vented to the outside, make sure the vent flapper opens up completely when the fan is running. You will see the vent flapper open when the fan is on. This will not be visible if the fan vents through the roof. This prevents cooking odors from filtering into the home.

- Where is the key for the garbage disposal? What is the key for?

- Open all cabinet doors and drawers to ensure they operate properly. (With the door of the cabinet closed, tap on the outside of the cabinet door on the side that opens to see if it bounces against the frame. It should fit snugly against the frame, if it doesn't, it needs adjusting.)

- Run the water at the faucet to check the water pressure as well as under the sink for any leaks.

Reminder: **Bold** and *italicized* words are defined in the back of this book.

Living/Dining Room

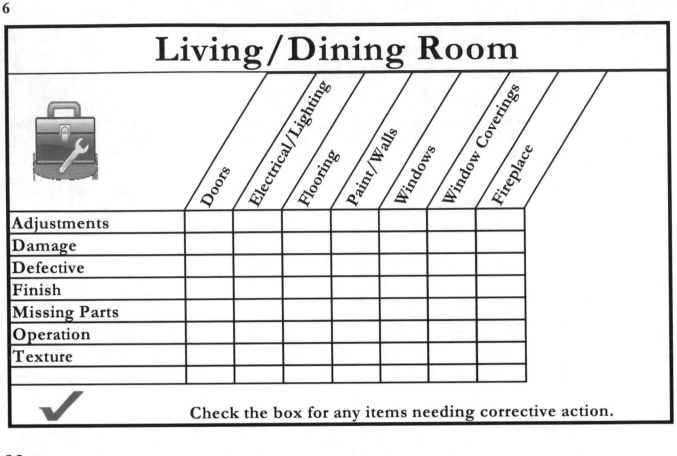

	Doors	Electrical/Lighting	Flooring	Paint/Walls	Windows	Window Coverings	Fireplace
Adjustments							
Damage							
Defective							
Finish							
Missing Parts							
Operation							
Texture							

Check the box for any items needing corrective action.

Notes:

Living/Dining Room:

- Is the texture on the walls and ceilings uniform in appearance? No noticeable repairs or *flashing of paint*?

- Do the doors open properly and close securely and lock? (You should not see any light coming from around the *exterior doors* when closed. Interior doors should open and close with ease and shut/lock securely.)

- Are there *GFCI's*?

- What is the *GFCI's* function?

- Use your nightlight to check each outlet to ensure it is working properly.

- Do all lights work (no burned out bulbs)?

- Do the *windows* slide open and close easily?

- Do the *windows* lock and unlock easily?

- Are window coverings installed and operating correctly?

- Are the *storm windows* and/or screens installed on the windows?

- Is the house *pre-wired for alarm* at exterior doors and windows? If so, do you see the *pre-wire alarm* button? If missing, have it noted on the chart as well as your builder/seller's paperwork for correction.

- Is the flooring free of any defects? (Refer to page 24—25 for more information)

- Are there any outlets operated by a *electrical wall switch*, which are called a *half hot*?

- If so, which part of the outlet (top or bottom) is connected to the *electrical wall switch*? This should be consistent throughout the home. Use your nightlight to check function.

- Do you have ceiling fans; if so, do they operate correctly and are they properly balanced? If the fan has a 10' extensions, proper balancing may not be possible. Are there remotes for the fans?

- If no fans, which *electrical wall switch* operates the *J-Box* on the ceiling?

- Locate thermostat and get instructions on programming the unit.

- Where are the air filters located? What are the sizes of the air filters?

- Where is the *FAU* (Forced Air Unit) located?

- How does the fireplace operate?

Reminder: **Bold** and *italicized* words are defined in the back of this book.

8

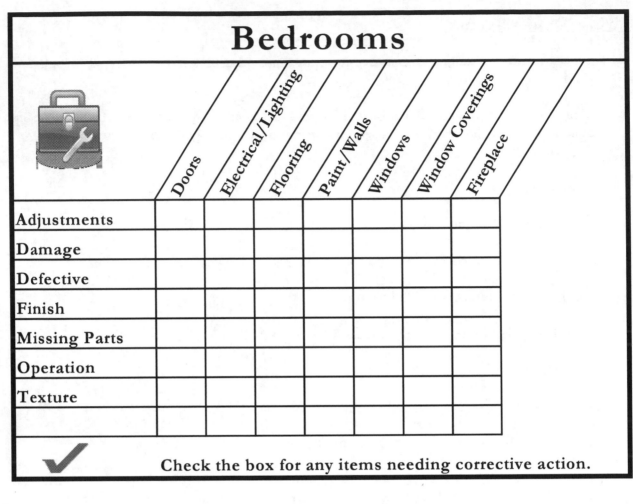

Bedrooms

	Doors	Electrical/Lighting	Flooring	Paint/Walls	Windows	Window Coverings	Fireplace
Adjustments							
Damage							
Defective							
Finish							
Missing Parts							
Operation							
Texture							

Check the box for any items needing corrective action.

Notes:

_____

_____

_____

_____

_____

_____

_____

_____

Bedrooms:

- Is the texture on the walls and ceilings uniform in appearance? No noticeable repairs or *flashing of paint*?

- Do the doors open properly and close securely and lock?   (You should not see any light coming from around the *exterior doors* when closed. Interior doors should open and close with ease and shut/lock securely. Verify you have the *door pin* to unlock any interior doors.)

- Use your nightlight to check each outlet to ensure it is working properly.

- Do all lights work (no burned out bulbs)?

- Do the *windows* slide open and close easily?

- Do the *windows* lock and unlock easily?

- Are window coverings installed and operating correctly?

- Are the *storm windows* and/or screens installed on the windows?

- Is the house *pre-wired for alarms* at exterior doors and windows? If so, do you see the *pre-wire alarm* button? If missing, have it noted on the chart as well as your builder/seller's paperwork for correction.

- Is the flooring free of any defects? (Refer to page 24—25 for more information)

- Are there any outlets operated by a *electrical wall switch*, which are called *half hots*?

- If so, which part of the outlet (top or bottom) is connected to the *electrical wall switch*? This should be consistent throughout the home. Use your nightlight to check function.

- Do you have ceiling fans; if so, do they operate correctly and are they properly balanced? Are there remotes for the fans?

- If no fans, which *electrical wall switch* operates the *J-Box* (if applicable) on the ceiling?

- Are there smoke detectors and/or CO2 smoke detectors? How are they powered and is there a back up system if you have a power outage?

Bathrooms

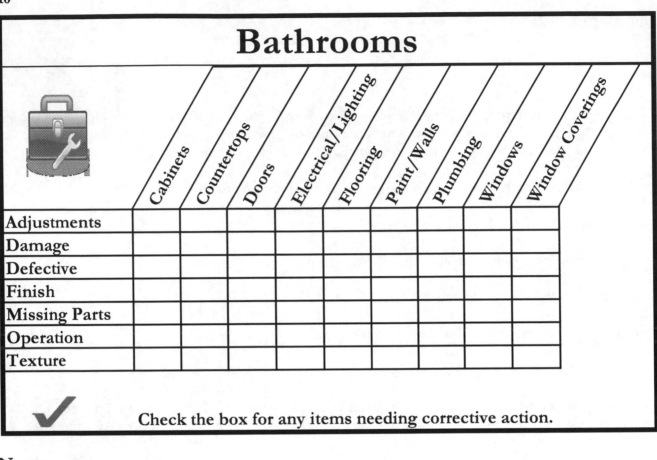

	Cabinets	Countertops	Doors	Electrical/Lighting	Flooring	Paint/Walls	Plumbing	Windows	Window Coverings
Adjustments									
Damage									
Defective									
Finish									
Missing Parts									
Operation									
Texture									

Check the box for any items needing corrective action.

Notes:

_____

_____

_____

_____

_____

_____

_____

_____

Bathrooms:

- Is the texture on the walls and ceilings uniform in appearance? No noticeable repairs or *flashing of paint*?

- Do the doors open properly and close securely and lock? (You should not see any light coming from around the *exterior doors* when closed. Interior doors should open and close with ease and shut/lock securely. Verify you have the *door pin* to unlock any interior doors.)

- Are there *GFCI's*?

- What is the *GFCI's* function?

- Use your nightlight to check each outlet to ensure it is working properly.

- Do all lights work (no burned out bulbs)?

- Does the *exhaust fan* work properly?

- Do the *windows* slide open and close easily?

- Do the *windows* lock and unlock easily?

- Are window coverings installed and operating correctly?

- Are the *storm windows* and/or screens installed on the windows?

- Is the house *pre-wired for alarms* at exterior doors and windows? If so, do you see the *pre-wire alarm* button? If missing, note it on the chart as well as on your builder/seller's paperwork for correction.

- Is the flooring free of any defects? (Refer to page 24 –25 for more information)

- Check the countertops for any defects.

- Run the water at the faucet to check the water pressure as well as under the sink for any leaks. Pull the stopper up on the sinks and tubs to ensure it holds water. Inspect the tub for chips or scratches.

- Is the hot and cold water on the proper side? (hot on left and cold on right)

- Does the toilet flush completely?

- Open all cabinet doors and drawers to ensure they operate properly, (With the door of the cabinet closed, tap on the outside of the cabinet door on the side that opens to see if it bounces against the frame. It should fit snugly against the frame, if it doesn't, it needs adjusting.)

- Inspect mirrors and medicine cabinets for defects.

Reminder: **Bold** and *italicized* words are defined in the back of this book.

12

Laundry Room

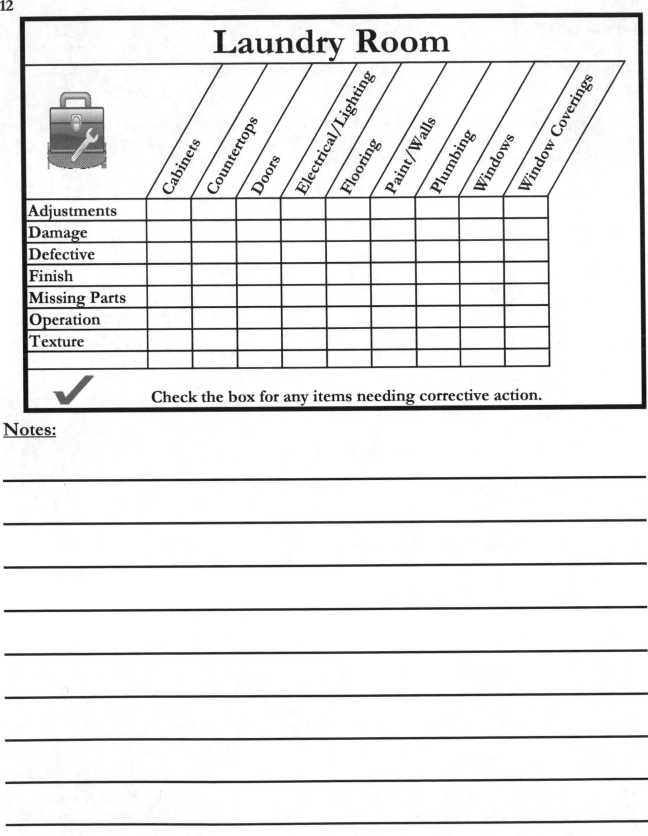

	Cabinets	Countertops	Doors	Electrical/Lighting	Flooring	Paint/Walls	Plumbing	Windows	Window Coverings
Adjustments									
Damage									
Defective									
Finish									
Missing Parts									
Operation									
Texture									

Check the box for any items needing corrective action.

Notes:

_____

_____

_____

_____

_____

_____

_____

_____

_____

_____

Laundry Room:

- Is the texture on the walls and ceilings uniform in appearance? No noticeable repairs or *flashing of paint*?

- Do the doors open properly and close securely and lock? (You should not see any light coming from around the *exterior doors* when closed. Interior doors should open and close with ease and shut/lock securely.)

- Are there *GFCI's*?

- What is the *GFCI's* function?

- Use your nightlight to check each outlet to ensure it is working properly.

- Do all lights work (no burned out bulbs)?

- Does the *exhaust fan* work properly?

- Do the *windows* slide open and close easily?

- Do the *windows* lock and unlock easily?

- Are window coverings installed and operating correctly?

- Are the *storm windows* and/or screens installed on the windows?

- Is the house *pre-wired for alarms* at exterior doors and windows? If so, do you see the *pre-wire alarm* button? If missing, have it noted on the chart as well as your builder/seller's paperwork for correction.

- Is the flooring free of any defects? (Refer to page 24—25 for more information)

- Check the countertops for any defects.

- If washer and dryer are provided, turn them on for a cycle to ensure proper operation (no vibrating or shaking and check proper drainage of both washer and venting of dryer to outside).

- Are the warranty manuals and registration cards for the appliances supplied?

- Locate the gas shut off valve for the dryer (unless electric).

- If the dryer is electric, does it have a 220 volt outlet?

- Open all cabinet doors and drawers to ensure they operate properly. (With the door of the cabinet closed, tap on the outside of the cabinet door on the side that opens to see if it bounces against the frame. It should fit snugly against the frame, if it doesn't, it needs adjusting.)

- If a laundry sink is installed, run the water to check the water pressure and under the sink for any leaks.

Reminder: **Bold** and *italicized* words are defined in the back of this book.

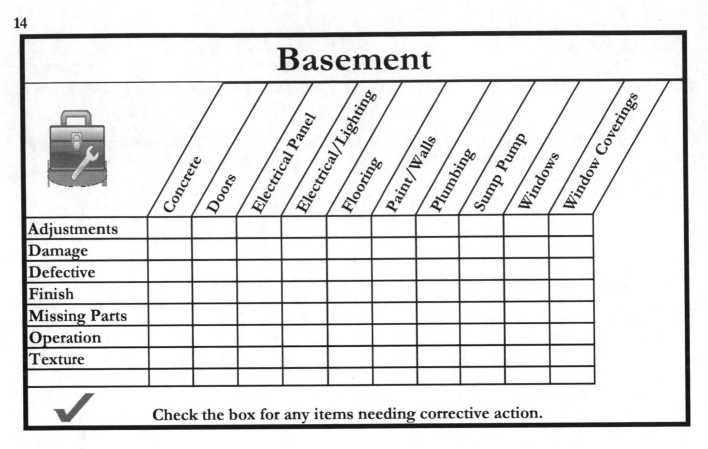

Basement

	Concrete	Doors	Electrical Panel	Electrical/Lighting	Flooring	Paint/Walls	Plumbing	Sump Pump	Windows	Window Coverings
Adjustments										
Damage										
Defective										
Finish										
Missing Parts										
Operation										
Texture										

Check the box for any items needing corrective action.

Notes:

Basement/Crawl Space:

- Is the texture on the walls and ceilings uniform in appearance? No noticeable repairs or *flashing of paint*?

- Are the walls dry and no noticeable water staining? If not, ensure proper drainage away from the house.

- Does the basement have a *sump pump*? Identify the drain exit to ensure water drains away from exterior foundation. When was it last serviced or installed?

- Examine all visible plumbing pipes for any leaks.

- If there is a bathroom run the water to check the water pressure and under sink for any leaks, (i.e., toilet, sink and shower).

- Do the doors open properly and close securely and lock? (You should not see any light coming from around the *exterior doors* when closed. Interior doors should open and close with ease and shut/lock securely.)

- Are there *GFCI's*?

- What is the *GFCI's* function?

- Use your nightlight to check each outlet to ensure it is working properly.

- Do all lights work (no burned out bulbs)?

- Does the *exhaust fan* work properly?

- Where is the electrical *sub-panel* or main electrical panel located?

- Do the *windows* slide open and close easily?

- Do the *windows* lock and unlock easily?

- Are the *storm windows* and/or screens installed on the windows?

- Is the house *pre-wired for alarms* at exterior doors and windows? If so, do you see the *pre-wire alarm* button? If missing, note it on the chart as well as your builder/seller's paperwork for correction.

- Is the flooring free of any defects? (Refer to page 24—25 for more information)

- Check the countertops for any defects.

- Open all cabinet doors and drawers to ensure they operate properly. (With the door of the cabinet closed, tap on the outside of the cabinet door on the side that opens to see if it bounces against the frame. It should fit snugly against the frame, if it doesn't, it needs adjusting.)

Reminder: **Bold** and *italicized* words are defined in the back of this book.

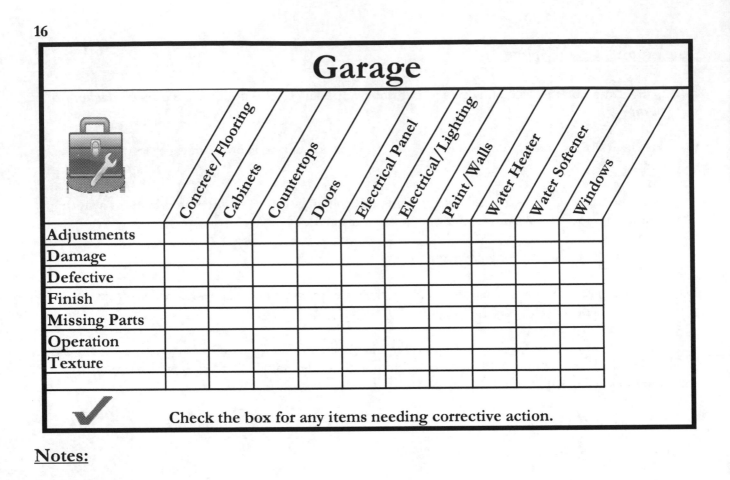

Garage

	Concrete/Flooring	Cabinets	Countertops	Doors	Electrical Panel	Electrical/Lighting	Paint/Walls	Water Heater	Water Softener	Windows	
Adjustments											
Damage											
Defective											
Finish											
Missing Parts											
Operation											
Texture											

Check the box for any items needing corrective action.

Notes:

_____

_____

_____

_____

_____

_____

_____

_____

_____

Garage:

- Is the texture on the walls and ceilings uniform in appearance? No noticeable repairs or *flashing of paint*?

- Do the doors open properly and close securely and lock? (You should not see any light coming from around the *exterior doors* when closed. Interior doors should open and close with ease and shut/lock securely.)

- Are there *GFCI's*?

- What is the *GFCI's* function?

- Use your nightlight to check each outlet to ensure it is working properly.

- Do all lights work (no burned out bulbs)?

- Do the *windows* slide open and close easily?

- Do the *windows* lock and unlock easily?

- Are the *storm windows* and/or screens installed on the windows?

- Is the house *pre-wired for alarms* at exterior doors and windows? If so, do you see the *pre-wire alarm* button? If missing, have it noted on the chart as well as your builder/seller's paperwork for correction.

- Is the flooring free of any defects? (Refer to page 24—25 for more information)

- Does the overhead garage door open and close smoothly?

- Are there proper safety features that are connected to the garage door opener?

- Check the remotes to make sure they are operational.

- Is the pilot light lit for the gas/electric water heater?

- Check the electrical *sub-panel*, are the circuit breakers properly labeled? Your home may have additional *sub-panels* located in other rooms such as a closet, basement or exterior.

- Is the *main water shut off valve* located within the garage? If so, does the handle move freely?

- Is the house plumbed for a soft water system?

- If soft water system is installed, make sure unit is on and programmed.

- Is there a landscape irrigation clock? Is it programmed correctly?

Reminder: **Bold** and *italicized* words are defined in the back of this book.

Exterior

	Concrete	Doors	Electrical Panel	Electrical/Lighting	Landscaping	Plumbing	Roof	Siding/Stucco	Windows	Walls/Fence	Gates	Screens
Adjustments												
Damage												
Defective												
Finish												
Missing Parts												
Operation												
Texture												

Check the box for any items needing corrective action.

Notes:

_____

_____

_____

_____

_____

_____

_____

_____

_____

Exterior:

- Are the exterior surfaces consistent in appearance or finish? No noticeable cracks, repairs or *flashing of paint* ?

- Do all lights work (no burned out bulbs)?

- Do the doors open properly and close securely and lock?   (You should not see any light coming from around the *exterior doors* when closed).

- Do the *concrete/decorative concrete* driveway, walk ways and patios have a uniform finish?

- Where are the *property lines*? Are they marked ?

- Is there a water shut off valve for the landscaping ?

- Are the water lines for the irrigation insulated for the above ground pipes?

- Where are the *utility meters* and *shut off valves* for the home (gas, water, electric)?

- Does the electrical main panel cover close correctly and lock in place?

- Are the *window weep holes* open and free of any blockage?

- Are the screens/*storm windows* installed and free of defects?

- How do you remove the screens/*storm windows* ?

- Is the *roofing material* laying flat? (No raised or missing materials, curled or warped skylights).

- Are there *vent stacks*?

- Are the gutters/downspouts in place and secure? Do they drain away from the house?

- Is the *hose spigot* secure in the wall? (Try moving the hose spigot; it should not move back and forth, if it does it needs to be secured to the framing of the house).

- Where are the *primary and secondary air conditioner condensate lines* located?

- Are there cracks or chips in the masonry walls? If so, repair or replace as needed.

- If metal fencing; check for paint finish and/or broken or bent rails on the fence.

- Does the gate open and close correctly?

- Is there proper drainage away from the foundation of the house?

Reminder: **Bold** and *italicized* words are defined in the back of this book.

Warranties and Manuals

It is important to remember to ask your builder or the seller if they have the warranties or manuals that correspond to the functionality of the appliances, pools, spas etc. of the house for your records.

Contact your builder for any warranty issues that arise. We recommend emailing them and clearly stating the issue or call the service representative directly. Even if you have an issue that is not covered under their warranty, it could result over time to be an existing condition that may be covered. Just remember to keep records on your investment, as it will pay off in the long run.

Some builders will supply a list of the trade contractors and their telephone numbers who were used to construct your new home. Please ask for one if you didn't receive one.

We recommend that you purchase a three-ring binder to hold all the warranty information on your home, since this is the beginning of your new adventure. This binder will ensure you have everything in one convenient place such as warranty books, manuals and anything else you deem important regarding your new home. Reminder...this would be a great place to include the copy of your *sub-panel* labels for future reference.

This following list may not include uncommon options you selected for your home through the builder/seller.

Here is a list of warranties and manuals that you should receive or request from your builder or seller. (Check upon receipt)

☐ A/C Condenser

☐ Association Codes, Covenants and Restrictions

☐ Builder Warranty Manual on all aspects of your new house. If you are purchasing a resale home, inquire with the seller on the availability of an outside warranty.

☐ Dishwasher

☐ Fireplace

☐ Flooring warranties (i.e., wood floor, carpet, tile, vinyl etc.)

☐ Garage Door Openers

☐ Garbage Disposal

☐ Heating (Known as FAU)/Air Conditioning Unit/Heat Pumps/Swamp Cooler

☐ Landscape Irrigation System

☐ Microwave

☐ Oven/Range/Refrigerator

☐ RO (Reverse Osmosis) System

☐ Smoke Detector and/or Carbon Monoxide Detector

☐ Thermostat

☐ Washer/Dryer

☐ Water Features (sink, faucets etc.)

☐ Water Heater

☐ Water Softener

☐ Window Coverings (if purchased through the builder/seller)

Cosmetic Deficiencies

Typically this warranty is for anything the builder considers to be something the homeowner could have damaged (i.e., countertops, flooring, windows, mirrors, door handles, doors, plumbing back-up). We suggest that once you move in you closely look at and make sure things work as intended. Once again, sewer back ups are normally only a 30-Day warranty, so run the water on the day of your walk through in the different locations, which will allow the water to drain from multiple areas into the plumbing system. Also, check with your builder as to how long their cosmetic deficiency warranty is.

Concrete

- *Concrete*: Does two things; it hardens and cracks. Concrete can take up to 20 years to fully cure. If concrete is heaving or has excessive cracking, consult your builder or a licensed concrete company.

- *Exterior decorative concrete:* To extend the life and beauty of your decorative concrete, you will need to perform routine maintenance by applying a sealer. The sealer protects the concrete from staining and enriches the final color. Consult a licensed concrete company.

Doors

- *Door Pin:* This is used to unlock bedroom and bathroom doors that are accidentally locked. We recommend storing the door pin on top of the door frame for easy accessibility should you need to use it.

- *Exterior doors:* Should be weather tight and the deadbolt lock should engage in the frame of the door. If it does not engage into the frame of the door this can be easily fixed. Close the door and sight where the deadbolt hits the strike plate in the door frame. Open the door and file the edge of the strike plate that it hits. Check every once and awhile to see if the deadbolt engages properly.

Italicized Words continued ...

Electrical/Lighting

- *Electrical Wall Switch* : In rooms that have multiple wall switches, you should understand what switch operates each component in the room (i.e., the first switch may operate the half hot, the second switch may operate the J-Box in the ceiling and so on). The wall switch order should be consistent throughout your home, if not, request that they be changed.

- *Exhaust Fan:* An exhaust fan is normally required in a room where there aren't any windows that open up to let in fresh air. The purpose of the exhaust fan is to exhaust any build up of humidity in a room. Exhaust fans are usually located in bathrooms and laundry rooms.

- *GFCI's:* Ground Fault Circuit Interrupters are normally located where electrical outlets are located by a water source; such as kitchen, bathrooms, laundry rooms and garage. The GFCI acts like a mini-circuit breaker to prevent shock and shorting out appliances.

- *Half Hots:* Outlets that operate off a wall switch. This means that one part of the outlet is *tied into* the wall switch and the other has full power. Make sure these outlets are consistent with other outlets in the home. By this we mean that either the top or the bottom part of the outlet is operated by the switch and is the same throughout the house, which will make it easier for you to identify them in a room. Consistency is the key to a friendly home.

- *J-Box:* (Junction Box) Located on the ceiling and operated by a wall switch that is *tied into* the J-Box for future installation of a light or ceiling fan.

Italicized Words continued ...

Electrical/Lighting continued...

- ***Pre-Wired Alarms:*** This is when the builder has pre-drilled and pre-run wiring for an alarm system. The location for the pre-alarm system is on all exterior doors and windows that open. You will be able to identify them by a white button on the frame of the windows and doors. All the wiring usually terminates in a closet.

- ***Sub Panels:*** Usually located in the garage, utility room or basement. This is where the electrical circuit breakers are for all the electrical components of the home. All circuit breakers should be labeled with their location next to each circuit breaker. We recommend taking a digital picture or writing down the location of each circuit breaker as the writing may fade over time.

- ***Tied Into:*** Electrical switch or outlet that operates a specific component in a room. i.e., half hot, J-Box, fan, GFCI and breaker.

FAU

- ***FAU:*** (**F**orced **A**ir **U**nit) supplies the heat and cooling throughout the home.

Flooring

To ensure your flooring has been laid straight you can use the baseboard as a straight edge by sighting the pattern along the wall. This is important especially if you have wood, patterned carpet or tile flooring. The flooring should be aligned and be straight and true with the baseboard.

- ***Carpet Seams:*** This is where the carpet has been joined with another piece of carpet at doorways or in large rooms. Carpet normally comes in 12' width. Carpet seams should not be noticeable, but will vary depending on the type of carpet in your home.

- ***Grout:*** Should have an even appearance in color and texture.

Italicized Words continued ...

Flooring continued ...

- <u>*Grout Shading:*</u> This is when the grout has an uneven appearance, such as white or haze over it. Typically this can be corrected by cleaning with a grout cleaner or stain sealing.

- <u>**Remnants:**</u> Make sure you have remnants (extra flooring) that was installed in your home. These can be used for future repairs, if they are needed, thus ensuring the same dye lot or color match.

- <u>*Stain Sealing:*</u> This is a product that makes the grout uniform in appearance and seals the grout in one application. It can be obtained through a tile company or tile manufacturer. Sealing the grout is normally a homeowner responsibility, not the builder. We recommend stain sealing over clear sealer due to uniformity from stain. Follow manufacturer's instructions.

- <u>*Tile:*</u> The ANSI (American National Standards Institute) deems uneven tile to be more than 1/8". Inspect your tile to ensure it is free of defects (chips, cracks or uneven). Is the grout uniform in appearance (i.e., no holes or uneven shading of the grout)? Is the grout cracking along the baseboards? When you walk or tap on the tile does it sound hollow?

- <u>*Vinyl:*</u> No noticeable seams, curling, separation, discoloration, bubbles or debris under vinyl.

Hose Spigot (exterior faucet)

- A hose spigot should not extend more than 2" from the finished exterior surface. The reason for this is durability and lessens the likelihood of someone bumping into it and dislodging the water line in the exterior wall.

Italicized Words continued ...

Paint/Walls

Typically the walls in kitchens, bathrooms and laundry rooms are painted with semi-gloss paint.

- *__Flashing of Paint:__* This is when a repair was done on a wall or ceiling and you can see where the repair was. Usually only one coat of paint was used on the repair. Normally 1 or 2 more coats will be needed to ensure even paint coverage in appearance.

- *__Noticeable Repairs:__* There are many types of finishes on the interior walls and ceilings. Some of the different types are orange peel, knock down, skip trowel or smooth coat. You will be able to notice repairs as they will not completely match the surrounding area or finish.

- *__Paint Cut Lines:__* Should be straight from ceilings to walls, baseboards to walls and to the flooring.

- *__Paint Touch Up Kit:__* You should receive a paint touch up kit.

Primary/Secondary Condensate Lines

These lines drain any excess condensation that has built up at the FAU (Forced Air Unit). The primary condensate drain line is normally located on an exterior wall of the home just above the ground. The secondary condensate drain line is normally located above a window or eave. On hot and humid days, when your air conditioning is running you will notice condensation (water) dripping from the primary line, which is normal. Condensation (water) should never drip from the secondary line. If this happens, it means the primary line is blocked and would be considered an emergency type situation. You should contact your builder if under warranty or a licensed heating and air conditioning company for evaluation and repair.

Italicized Words continued ...

Property Lines

- **_Property Lines:_** Usually located at the street or curbing. It can be distinguished by a + (plus) sign. You may also obtain a plot plan of your property through the builder or City Planner.

Roofing Materials

- **_Roofing Material:_** Should be the same color and uniform throughout. Notify builder/seller for correction. Remember, curb appeal is the first impression of your home.

- **_Air Vents:_** Some roofs have what look like air vents laying on the roof. They are situated at various locations throughout the roof. These vents should be laying flat against the roofing material. Some homes will have gable vents, which are located under the eave. The purpose of such vents are to ventilate the attic area of the home.

- **_Vent Stacks:_** Are pipes that protrude through the roof which are required for proper function of your home, (i.e., water heater, plumbing and heating). Some of the vent stacks will have a cap on them. This signifies that they are related to either a gas appliance or fireplace.

Sump Pumps

- *Sump Pumps:* Located in the basement. Basement flooding is a common problem, particularly in houses situated on flat terrain where rain and snow melt have little chance for runoff. When the ground becomes saturated, ground water pressure builds, forcing water towards any path of least resistance. A sump pump is used to extract water from under the foundation by pumping to an exterior location. Because submersibles sit in water a good deal of the time, they can have a life span of from 5 to 15 years. Pedestals, on the other hand, may continue to operate for as long as 25 or 30 years. (Because a pump's life is closely related to the conditions and frequency of its use, most manufacturers offer limited 1-year warranties.)

Utility Meters

- *Main Electrical Panel:* This electrical panel houses the main shut off switch for the entire home (tied into the sub-panel).

- *Main Gas Shut Off Valve:* This valve is located at the gas meter.

- *Main Water Shut Off Valve:* This valve is usually located near the street or the front exterior of the house.

Windows

- Inspect window glass for scratches and defects from 10' in non-direct sunlight. If the window has a small defect that looks like a fish eye; (Θ) the window will need to be replaced as this is a manufacturer defect. If there are minor scratches, they can usually be buffed out. If the scratch is deep, the window will need to be replaced.

- Today, window glass is usually dual or triple paned, so the defect could be in between the glass.

Windows continued ...

- Inquire with builder/seller to see if your new home has low E glass in the windows. The E stands for emissivity. Low E glass works by reflecting heat back to its source. It does this by utilizing an ultra thin metallic coating on or in the glass. Windows with low E glass can help stop the loss of heat/cooling from your home as well as reduce condensation on the glass.

- **_Storm Windows:_** Exterior-mounted storm windows must have "weep holes" at the bottom of the frame to allow any moisture that collects between the primary window and the storm window to drain out. Even though these drainage holes subtract from energy savings, not having them will eventually cause the primary window frame to rot, and possibly make them impossible to operate.

- **_Window Weep Holes_**: The weep holes are located on the bottom corners of the exterior window frame. The weep holes allow water to drain from the interior window tracks. It is important that these weep holes are clear of debris at all times.

Quick ✔ Definitions

Adjustments:
1. Cabinet doors not level, loose hinges or hard to open.
2. Windows difficult to open.
3. Window locks difficult to operate.
4. Appliances need to be leveled or secured.
5. Doors that bind or do not close properly.

Damage:
1. Scratches on cabinets, countertops, mirrors, windows or appliances.
2. Bent screens.

Defective:
1. Something that does not operate properly or the way it is intended to operate.
2. Something that does not fit properly or binds.
3. Something that does not meet industry standards.

Finish:
1. Uneven paint coverage on walls, doors, ceilings or baseboards.

Missing Parts:
1. Window locks and slider locks at the bottom of the slider door.
2. Door bump at the baseboards to keep the door from hitting the wall.

Operation:
1. GFCI Outlets located in the kitchen and bathrooms.
2. Do all major components work properly? (i.e., appliances, FAU and water heater)
3. Run the water at all locations during your walk through, which will ensure unclogged plumbing lines.

Texture:
1. Uneven texture on walls or ceilings. (You will be able to see if the walls/ceilings were patched due to the inconsistency of the surrounding texture.)

Helpful Hints

A/C Filters: Change filters every 30 to 45 days to ensure optimum performance of your heating and air conditioning system.

Cabinets: Treat cabinets as you would your furniture. Apply a non-lemon based furniture polish to them regularly. Do not use lemon based furniture polish or an oil based polish as these may yellow your cabinets and affect the finish over time. Cabinets can dry out if not protected regularly.

Door Hinges: If hinges are squeaking when you open or close the door, the easiest way to repair this is by removing the hinge pin and apply a little Vaseline® to the pin and reinserting. You will need to listen to determine which pin is squeaking. If more than one hinge is squeaking, remove only one pin at a time.

Fire Extinguishers: We recommend having a fire extinguisher underneath the kitchen sink and in the garage.

Showers and Tubs: We recommend vacuuming along the tub and shower surrounds due to latex caulking used along these edges, which can become dirty during cleaning. By vacuuming these areas will ensure a clean and fresh appearance to your tub and shower surrounds.

Smoke Detectors/CO2 Detectors: Change batteries in each unit every year.

Tile and Grout: It is best to vacuum the tile and grout rather than using a broom or duster. The vacuum will lift the dirt off of the tile and grout, whereas a broom will push the dirt into the grout, thus making the grout dirtier faster. Use only clean water (change water as it becomes dirty) to mop tile floors once you have vacuumed them clean.

Window Tracks: Vacuum window tracks regularly due to dirt build up. Dirt built up will affect the performance of your windows over time. Once clean, spray a silicone lubricant onto the tracks to maintain functionality, slide the window open and closed to allow the lubricant to work over the rollers in the window. You should do this every three months. You will need to perform this same task on your sliding glass door track.

Maintenance Schedule

		Jan	Feb	Mar	Apr	May	June	July	Aug	Sept	Oct	Nov	Dec
Every 30 Days	Air Filters												
	Caulking Wet Locations												
	Door Hinges												
	Exhaust Fans												
	Ext. Door Weatherstripping												
	Exterior Lighting												
	Faucet Aerators												
	GFCI's												
	Landscape Sprinklers												
	Plumbing Lines												
	Rangehood Filters												
	Roof Tile												
	Tile Grout												
	Window Weep Holes												
Every 90 Days	Cabinets												
	Flooring												
	Garage Door												
	Windows												
Once Per Year	Exterior Surfaces												
	Landscape Clock												
	Smoke and CO2 Detectors												
	Water Heater												

Maintenance Schedule Tips

Every 30 Days

Air Filters

Change air filters. This will ensure your FAU (forced air unit) works at peak performance.

Caulking At Wet Locations

Check caulking around countertops and toilets and recaulk if necessary with a silicone based caulking.

Door Hinges

Check for ease of operation (squeaks) and/or a black residue at the hinge. This residue is a result of the hinge pin rubbing against the hinge. To eliminate this as well as any squeaks, lubricate one hinge pin at a time.

Exhaust Vents

Check exterior exhaust vents for obstruction. Remove any obstructions if necessary.

Ext. Door Weatherstripping

Check weatherstripping at all exterior doors. If necessary, repair or replace damaged weatherstripping to ensure no air leaks.

Exterior Lighting

Check all exterior lights (i.e., entry light, address light and rear patio lights) for operation. Replace burned out bulbs as needed.

Faucet Aerators

Each faucet in your home has an aerator, which is located at the end of the faucet. Over time, sediment can build up in the aerator, which diminishes your water pressure. Unscrew the aerator in a counter-clockwise direction and clean by rinsing and/or tapping gently to remove sediment.

GFCI's

Push TEST button to ensure operation. Push RESET button to reset outlet. If TEST button fails to pop out or reset, the outlet may be bad and need to be replaced by a licensed electrician.

Landscape Sprinklers

Check sprinkler heads and drip emitters for damage or clogs. Replace if necessary. Check the direction of the spray and adjust if necessary.

Plumbing Lines

Check under sinks and at toilets for water leaks. Usually you can tighten the plumbing lines if they are leaking, otherwise consult a licensed plumber.

Rangehood Filters

These are located above the stove. Remove filter, wash in warm soapy water and let dry.

Roof Tile

Visually check roof material from the ground. If you notice any roofing material that has lifted, consult a licensed roofing contractor to repair.

Tile Grout

Check grout for cracking along baseboards and throughout room. You may purchase a grout caulking product from a tile store. Verify the correct grout color before repairs. If the grout has been previously sealed, there may be a color variance. Allow 30 days for new grout to fully cure before applying sealer.

Maintenance Schedule Tips

Every 90 Days

Cabinets
Use a non-lemon oil based furniture polish to protect the cabinets and the finish. Clean cabinets if they are dirty or greasy with mild soap and water. Make sure to dry cabinets completely before applying furniture polish.

Flooring
Check flooring for any damage. Repair or replace as needed.

Garage Door
Use a silicone spray to lubricate the garage door hinges, springs, rollers and pull chain. Do not lubricate the opener chain as this could damage the garage door opener motor.

Windows/ Sliding Glass Doors
Vacuum window tracks to ensure rollers function properly. Lubricate clean window tracks with a silicone spray for smooth operation.

Once a Year

Exterior Surfaces
Wash the exterior surfaces of your home. Always start at the bottom of the structure and work your way up. This keeps the dirt moving freely off the surface of the home. If you have a two-story home you might need to use a pressure washer. By washing the exterior surfaces this will extend the product life of the materials on your home.

Landscape Clock
Check to ensure clock is properly set and replace batteries.

Smoke Detectors/ CO2 Detectors
Change batteries.

Water Heater
Due to hard water fine crystals/sediment can build up in the bottom of the water heater. Follow manufacturers instructions to drain the water heater or hire a licensed plumbing contractor.

Tools You Should Have in Your Tool Box

- Caulking (different types)

- Files or Rasps (various sizes and types)

- Flashlight

- Work Gloves

- Hammer

- Level

- Pliers (Crescent and Channel Locks)

- Plug Tester

- Putty Knives (two different sizes)

- Screwdrivers (Philips and Slotted)

- Silicone Spray

- Spackle

- Tape Measure

- Utility Knife

- First Aid Kit

Contact List

Gas/Propane Company Name:_____   Emergency Phone #_____

Account #_____   Phone #_____

Electric Company Name:_____   Emergency Phone #_____

Account #_____   Phone #_____

Water Company Name:_____   Emergency Phone #_____

Account #_____   Phone #_____

Garbage/Waste Company Name:_____   Emergency Phone #_____

Account #_____   Phone #_____

Telephone Company Name:_____   Emergency Phone #_____

Account #_____   Phone #_____

Insurance Company Name:_____   Emergency Phone #_____

Account #_____   Phone #_____

Security Company Name:_____   Emergency Phone #_____

Account #_____   Password:_____

Hospital/Doctor Name:_____   Phone #_____

Local Police Department:_____   Phone #_____

Local Fire Department:_____   Phone #_____

Plumber Name:_____   Phone #_____

Electrician Name:_____   Phone #_____

Other Key Contacts:

Name:_____   Phone #_____

Name:_____   Phone #_____

Name:_____   Phone #_____

NOTES:

NOTES:

NOTES:

Printed in the United States
by Baker & Taylor Publisher Services